THE **TALKING WALL**

THE MISSING

MAUSILEE JACKSON

THE TALKING WALL
THE MISSING

iUniverse books may be ordered through booksellers or by contacting:

iUniverse
1663 Liberty Drive
Bloomington, IN 47403
www.iuniverse.com
1-800-Authors (1-800-288-4677)

Because of the dynamic nature of the Internet, any web addresses or links contained in this book may have changed since publication and may no longer be valid. The views expressed in this work are solely those of the author and do not necessarily reflect the views of the publisher, and the publisher hereby disclaims any responsibility for them.

Any people depicted in stock imagery provided by Getty Images are models, and such images are being used for illustrative purposes only. Certain stock imagery © Getty Images.

ISBN: 978-1-5320-7942-9 (sc)
ISBN: 978-1-5320-7941-2 (e)

Library of Congress Control Number: 2019910706

Print information available on the last page.

iUniverse rev. date: 07/30/2019

Look at her, getting ready to cook dinner like nothing happen. Always ready to do the right thing as if nothing ever happens in her life. That man of hers is no good to her. She knows it, but she keeps an open mind as if all will be well someday.

I hope that her day comes soon. I do not know how much more she can bear. Thank you, I am not human, because the life she lives would have been over a decade ago. This woman is amazing to do whatever this man says. He tells her what to do, as if she does not have a mind of her own. He tells her how and what to cook. If it were I, I would tell him to cook for his self.

I wish people knew the truth about what goes on in this house. No one ever would believe her if she could tell it. People look at the wealth a person has and not the emotion that person is feeling. I feel your pain, somewhat and I know what is happening to you. I just wish I could do something.

I tell you this man has no knowledge. He does not want to do any extracurricular or have any hobby for that matter. If she mention of something she wants to do outside of the home he would get upset. However, he will work, when he is called to worked. He can however be a slicker if you really paid attention to him. The atmosphere has some how put these two together for an unknown reason. They started out great but his love for money soon became known. Missy, who is an attorney for a very well known law firm, like to volunteer at different charities and political functions. Her love for law became very clear after two years of college.

Mausilee Jackson

2

There are times when this house gets no peace some nights. This man can start trouble just by opening his eyes. He argues about salt and pepper if he looked at it long enough. He does what ever he wants to do. He can buy whatever he want without even discussing it with her. She, on the other hand, has to ask. She even has to show him the receipt if she spends his money. There have been times when the two of them argued over a bill and bills have to be paid, but no way was he going to do it. I wish I had hands I would hit him upside his head. Occasionally I do knock things off the wall to draw the attention on something else.

Well, it is a beautiful day. I hope this day is a joyous one. Mister is up and in rare form, so much for joy. Missy got a new up-do, we will see if he notices. No, he did not. Why would he? He thinks less of her. Now if some one else show her a complement, he just frown. Oh what a husband he is.

When Sunday comes the sun will shine on Missy and give her a good day. Only time can predict what will happen with these two. This marriage is something else. No one knows it, but the atmosphere has its way of helping when we do not know it. He on the other hand could care less. He has gotten to the point, as it seem to me, that he does not care for her any more. He rather bet on the games and flash money at the Ladies. Missy is a trophy for him.

3

He was thinking about running for Mayor, since he sits on the City Council Board, then notice he had no woman that he could call his "wife". His friends decided to help him. Friends of friends introduced Mister to Missy and the relationship grew from there. He has no common sense, yet he is a very smart and intelligent young man. At times it seems as if he is the only one on this earth. The way he brag on himself. He says how he will changed the world one day. If you asked me, I think he created himself with all that pride sitting on his shoulder. If pride would win a prize, he would win for sure. His head is so far in the cloud he cannot see anything but the stars around the earth.

Oh, I feel so for this beautiful woman given to Mister with the help of silly friends. I wish I knew the reason. I only know my purpose. I am to protect the ones who live under and between me. I am a hanging tree for old photos. I collect dust you cannot see. I hear everything said to you. I know where you hide your most precious valuables. I can protect you from the wind, rain, snow and sleet, even hot sunshine. I cannot however, protect you from the love ones that hurt you. I love my duty for humanity, but sometimes it makes me so angry. I can do so much, but I do so little to help you defend yourself.

Mausilee Jackson

Have no fear my friend, one day you will come to realize you have the power to do amazing things. He will see you shine without his help. Just keep pushing.

On live stream this morning, Dr. Minister Child Johnson said

4

"Continue". Yes, that is a great word. Continue knowing that not all is lost. You will one day have the victory.

Oh what a beautiful morning, the sun is shining so bright this morning. Breakfast smells all over the house. The weather is great and, oh, no he did not! He called her a Whore! What? This poor woman does all she can to maintain her faithfulness to him. Even after all the other women and men, he has had since the marriage. Right here in their home. Mister says all the time this is his house, he can not stand the fact that she is part owner as well. He asked her to take her name off the deeds but Missy would not give in. A Whore is she. I swear. I hope she show him what one really is. So to speak.

He has not had sex with her for a while and she remains faithful to his no good for nothing. She cooks and cleans even when she is ill. He got his nerves. I, I, I cannot stand him anymore! I am just boiling inside. I should make a pipe burst, break something. Nah, he just blame it on her. That low down, dirty, cheating, oh, I could go on, but what is the use.

I have been watching her closely. She looks as if something is wrong with her. She comes from a line of women that do not take much for long. Italian women are no push over. Missy birth name was Bambi, meaning Little Girl. Her parents changed it before their move to the United States. Her parents wanted to make sure their child had an American name as to live the American dream without being teased. She just decided to be safe and live an enormous life like most New Yorkers. He just crossed the line this time. When it hit him, watch out world. I am afraid Mister will pay dearly for this. She has

covered her life so well, that people think her marriage is all that. Some even wish for her life.

Something defiantly is wrong with her. She been coming and going and staying out until dark, this is out of character for her. She's been cooking, cleaning and saying nothing. Tomorrow we will see what happens.

Oh, did I miss anything today? Well, she did not fix breakfast this morning. Missy is mobile, as she has always been for the last two weeks. No food has been cooked today. Maybe Missy will bring dinner home. Oh, well.

Missy has never acted liked this, she has always been so carefree and forgiven. I notice Missy conduct has changed; she loved to talk to Mister when he got home, now she could care less.

Missy goes to bed early just to keep from talking to Mister. When he goes to bed, she gets up. Oh, that is not good. That is not the way to handle things. You must talk it out.

Oh, I wish she could hear me. I got it. I will push the candles off the wall. She does not like them anyway. Maybe she will ask Mister to pick them up for her. No, she would not do that. Her wound is deep this time. There are things in a marriage you just do not do. Calling your wife a Whore is one of them. How can a husband let that come out of his mouth? My answer is he does not care. His mom maybe did not show him how to care for a Lady. If he cared, or loved her truly, nothing in the world would have let such a word like that come out of his mouth, even if somebody had a gun to his head.

6

From what I have gathered, love carries a significant amount of weight and nothing can out-weigh love. I did not know he was so naive, so inconsiderate of others. So inconsiderate of his wife, the woman who said "I do" to a man she loved. He just wants to look good and gain all the glory as if he were a god. Maybe he will take her out to dinner. That will help ease the pain.

Well another day has come and gone. Missy is still not talking to Mister. I have not heard her or him say a word. She has not been going out for dinner either. She has really changed. I have notice it, so why does he not see what is happening?

Oh, I forget he does not pay her any attention. He does not even notice when she get her haircut. What man would not notice from down to your knees to shoulder length hair? Oh to be a man like he. I am so proud to be a wall. Mister mentioned a few months ago, that he was giving her a gift for Christmas. Well, Christmas is here, and I see no gifts under the tree. So I guess what he gave her was NOTHING ! I will say it again NOTHING !

You thought he would spend money on her. He would rather wrap up something from around the house. She was not surprise, it happens every year. Being married for twelve years, she knows not to look forward to receiving a gift from him.

It's this time of the year she think about what her life would have been like if she had not miss the opportunity to marry her first love. Oh how she talks about it to her best friend Brittany. Missy says it must not have been meant to be. She ask friends about him from time to time.

7

She prays to God, to take away the memory so it will not come between her marriage. She does not want to be unfaithful to her husband no matter how he does.

The New Year will be a grand year I predict. Missy has plans that do not involve the Mister, but if he wants to join in, she would not stop him. Oh how she wanted to be a Community Organizer. She just wants to give back time to people that need time. There is a lot on her plate for the New Year. I looked at her notes one night while she was watching television. I hope she pulls it through. If she prays and fast as she said, she would, then it would block the obstacles that Mister has in store for her. Yes, I believe he plans for her failure. He likes to be on the top. Whenever they are in a situation where Missy is getting complements and praises he just turn blue with anger.

He turns all eyes on something else, sometimes himself.

She is sad today for some reason. I have never seen her like this. Did Mister do something? How? I have not been asleep. She drinks a cup of tea and prays. Tears fall from her face. Oh how I wish I could help. I am looking around but I see no sign of trouble. I see where nothing happen in the night. She prays again, oh I see, it is someone birthday. Who? She cries again.

Well, Mister is up and in a good mood. A great day it may be. Missy cooks breakfast and watch television. Mister goes to sleep again. He must not be well, this is not like him. Missy goes in to check on him. He is breathing, so he is okay. She often would check his forehead to make sure he was all right, but now she just makes sure he is alive.

8

Well, no one knows for sure what happens between these walls. His so-called friends think he is so grand of a person. I better not think about Mister as a negative person. Negative thinking represents a negative atmosphere, so I hear.

Oh my, Missy has had enough. They have been arguing and I did not hear it. She tells Mister she is leaving and Mister pretends to be okay with it. Mister say, "Leave. I do not need you." "You have hung around long enough. I can handle my life by myself." Then he leaves. I hope Missy is gone before he returns. Mister was mad like a dog with rabies.

She, at first stare out the window, as she watches Mister drives off. Missy says, "Okay let's get going". Missy packs the things she can grab in a hurry. She takes the Tablet, her favorite book by Kay Arthur; "Lord I need grace to make it." She also takes a blanket she made years ago. It is not a pretty blanket, but it is the only thing she has left that her hands made and it makes her feel safe. Her clothes are already packed. Missy is smart she packed those months ago. Okay she is ready to go. Okay, take a deep breath, and out the door she goes. Finally, peace has entered the heart of a Woman who has bored more than some animals in the wild. She will make it. The atmosphere is just right for this time. She will be missed. Mister will see what a "Grand Woman" he drove away.

Well Mister made it through the week by his self. To my surprise he did not call Missy everyday the first two weeks. Now he calls every other day, but I don't hear him saying anything. I guess Missy does

not answer the phone. I hope he will see he needs Missy to help him make it. If she comes back, I hope he become the man and husband she need to have.

Well ninety-three days has passed and suddenly the phone rings. It's Missy. Oh my land, she called. Mister answers the phone and a conversation is going on. He let her talk and then to my surprise, Mister Say, "I'm sorry for all I've done." I guess she accepted cause the next morning, Missy was cooking breakfast. Well I'm bleeding inside but I hope all works out for these two. They both have had a chance to get their mind correct and think of the goals they have planned in the first year of marriage.

Sometimes I think Mister has forgotten the goals. He wake up and what ever his mind say do, that is the order for the day.

Oh how I wish the best for them. They will make it. I will try to see to it that they do, if they pay attention. I have notice that Missy has changed her routine a little. She does yoga and gardening early in the morning. I guess she is trying to be healthier. I have not seen Mister for a while. I wonder where he is. Believe you me, he is somewhere near by. Even thou they fuss and fight like wolves; they are hardly apart for a very long time. He cannot sleep without her by his side. Oh I forget. He may be on a business trip. He sometimes get orders in the middle of the night from the company he is managing. Oh well he will not be gone long.

10

I have notice the garden is becoming very beautiful. I have never seen sunflowers with such a giant head and sturdy stalks. They seem to salute as the wind blows. The dirt in the flower pots in the kitchen even look different, a soft, strange texture looking soil, black color with a rich texture. I notice Missy use the same dirt for all the houseplants and they have never been so lovely. The aloe plants are so full of vigor and vibrant. The aloe seems to say, "See me. Here I am."

"Oh what a peaceful night I had." says Missy. It was restful, even I the wall got some shut-eye. The atmosphere feels crisp and fresh; actually, it feels like the calm before the storm. WOW! Look at Missy, her hair is flowing like a rice crop on a breezy summer day. Never saw her look so awake this early in the morning.

The tea is steeping and the aroma is heavenly. Missy is cooking breakfast. I guess Mister has already eaten. Missies sit and eat while reading a book by one of her other favorite authors, Maya Angelou. Oh, how Missy is glowing and enjoying every bite. She is in heaven right now. Missy turns on some music and dances around the kitchen for a while. She seem so relax as if to be having an out of body experience. She twirls, twists and sways, then in an instinct she hugs herself as if to say, "I love me."

Oh no, a look of fear comes upon her face. Wonder what is happening? Missy does not look so good right now. Isn't it funny how things change from minute to minute. Is something strange going on here?

11

Missy is too kind-hearted to think ugly thoughts of anyone. She is done eating now. She stares out the kitchen window. I see on her face she is not right. Maybe she is pondering on how she and Mister fell in love. He would give her flowers in the middle of the night knowing she had to get up by five am, but loving her was all he had on his mind.

Then there was another side no one knew. Mister would sleep all day so he could stay up and vacuum late at night to piss Missy off. But she did not mind, she acted as if nothing happened.

I know she is raging inside. Even a dog can only take so much.

What is she doing? Is Missy talking to herself? I see no one is in the house. Is she losing her mind? WHAT!

"Oh you think you're so smart. Nope, you cannot bring me down anymore! I have gotten rid of you once and for all. You think you can come back. Oh no, I will not let that happen.

No, no, stop it! You cannot talk to me anymore. You are not here. You can't return. Do you think you can come back? No friend, not in this lifetime.

Oh, a whore am I? I cook your dinner, wash your clothes, and give you my paycheck. I was faithful to your cheating behind. No more slaving from this Chic. I was stuck with you because I was hoping to make a difference in the our life and maybe in the world.

You conning no good for nothing, you did not know anything about politics let alone being on the City Council. Yea, I got you where you belong now.

What trail? You are gone brother. No one will find out as soon as I get rid of some things around this house. No one will ever know. If I had been, a two-comma woman this marriage would still be on the up and up."

However, you no good for air could not keep your pants zipped and hands to your self. You are smart in books, but no sense God gave a worm.

Oh yea, you were some tycoon. Even had the Mayor fooled. The power you were given, gave you some prestige. Oil companies depended on you for advice. Even some Senators asked for advice. Man if they only knew.

I loved you with all my heart. The jealousy is what ruined the marriage. See jealousy is like salt in food. A little can enhance the savor, but too much can spoil the pleasure."

I hear Missy talking to herself. What is wrong with her? She looks horrible. What happen between breakfast and now? Her hair is all in disarray and bags under her eyes. Looks as if she has been in a fight. Why is she acting as if she is mentally ill? Maybe after having left Mister for a while Missy lost her mind. Mister will be back soon.

It seems as if the word that has been spoken in this house has somehow been buried in the walls. I believe a spirit has entered into Missy. She seem possessed with someone else mind.

Oh no, here comes Smokey, Mister's cat, with dirt all over his paws. Look at the dirt all over the kitchen floor that Missy cleaned last night.

Missy picks up Smokey and says, "I know where you've been.

Let's go get cleaned up." Missy cleans Smokey and feeds him, and then Missy goes and takes a shower. Later Missy sit down with a cup of tea. She watches Smokey play with a rock he brought in from outside. Missy wonders where he found that rock. There are no rocks in her yard; Missy does not like small rocks. Missy says; "Okay Smokey, you enjoy that rock tonight, in the morning it will be gone."

Smokey plays for a long time then off to bed he goes. The next morning Missy picks up the rock and put it on the counter by the back door, so she will remember to take it outside later that morning. Missy does her morning routine. Dance, yoga, meditation then breakfast. After breakfast, Missy cleans the kitchen. She forgets about the rock on the counter and takes out the trash.

Here comes Smokey with dirt on his paws again. Oh my, Missy will be mad as a hornet when she sees that. Missy comes in, she see the dirt Smokey brought in. Missy sweeps up Smokey puts him in the tub and clean him up. Missy does something different this time. She put Smokey in the cage, cleans up the kitchen, and sweeps the dirt in a dish and put the dirt in the big plant by the bay window in the living room. Missy goes into the den for a while, sits at her desk and works on a case.

Well the day has been very quiet. Mister has not called since he has been away this time. He must be on a very busy business trip. Well Missy has gotten plenty done. The floors are clean, all the dishes are washed and put away. The windows are so clean I can see the beauty of the trees.

14

Missy also put up new curtains in the living room, they are so beautiful.

What is that I hear? It is 2am. What could that be? Is Missy up? "Why are you bothering me? I curse the words planted on this ground surrounding the house I work so hard to maintain. I beat the words that have blocked my way to success. I break the chain that has held me down in a rout of despair and humiliation. I loved you with all my breath. I spent every waking hour loving you, but you did not care, your heart was closed. Only an open-heart can see the love I had. Your ego was so tall you could not see over it. I thought our love was perpetual. I do not think I could ever love another, after you raped me of my conscience, my well-being, my own self-worth. You drained every ounce of pride I had left. I would have giving you every cell in my body filled with love. The Olympus has fallen here. Married to you was like pitching camp in a lion's den. I never knew when you would attack. I had hoped my love was enough to change you. There is no space in the atmosphere that can hold the hatred I have for you now."

"I am every woman". No good man has every seen the good goods I have. I was willing to give it all to you. If only you would let me into your heart. If you are still here, let the doorknob hit you where the good Lord split you."

Missy goes to bedroom and slams the door. What a night she is having. She must be taking the wrong medication. The next morning she wakes talking to herself again. I hate to see her like this.

I assume she is missing Mister. He's stayed away this long before. Missy should be used to the alone time. Just listen to her, rambling

15

like a drunken person.

"Better yet, say hello to Ms. Karma. Remember all the things you have done to me. Remember all the words you said. Remember the bitter sweet. Karma will bring you back to your senses. Some people say we end up where we suppose to be. I believe I missed mine. When I had plans to have dinner with another love I had at that time, I skipped dinner and went to a movie with some friends instead.

I believed I change the course of time, therefore changing my destiny. Then I met you that night and I thought you were the one for me. I must had one too many before the movie.

Life can throw some curve balls. I fouled out when I said I do to you, only I did not know it. Maybe I can backtrack and then catch-up with the correct destiny longing for me. This time I will not get hurt nor will I hurt. I do not want to close another door on my life's chapter. When I see what is waiting for me I will run to it before it gets away. I am a champion and you're going to hear me roar."

"Mister, what kind of name is that? Your birth name was Angelo, meaning messenger. I wonder what message were you to give me? Your father Valentino, before moving to America, gave you the name Mister, meaning Superior to him. You tried to live up to that name. In America, you thought it would be easy to climb the ladder of success. You went to college and earned the degree your father told you to pursue, political science. Your father thought you could be President of United States one day, not knowing one had to be American-born, therefore, that dream was canceled. You went on to other things you thought you could swing at. You wanted to be a

Bellwether of an Oil company, but could not mustard the part. The ship you tried to sail docked before God parted the land from sea. Welcome to "Heartbreak Hotel." I hope your host was Ms. Karma."

"Yea, I remembered the days we use to love on each other and did not pay any heed to what time of day it was. Then after a while, it had to be dark and on a particular day of the week. Oh how things and people change."

"Seems as if after the marriage you stuck a key in my back and wounded me up whenever you needed me.

My life with you was like a rat running on an endless wheel, aiming for the cheese, not knowing I had to get off the wheel to get the cheese.

Therefore, Mister, here I stand. I am off the wheel of endless time. My aim is to bring my dream to life. Now MOVE! Get out of here! Walking behind you in this marriage, I collected many mileage points, so now it is time to cash them in. Like I said. I am a champion and you are going to hear me roar!"

"Do you hear me talking to you? Are you still here? You were here last night. I could not sleep for you turning the water on and off, opening the closet doors, and turning off the television. Come out, you no good for life!"

Oh my Lord, Missy needs help. I wonder what has gotten into her.

She looks as if she has been through a whirlwind. It is getting late and she has to work in the morning. I see she has gotten a cup of tea to calm her down. She will be okay after a good night of sleep.

I hope Mister will be home soon and she can be back to her old self.

17

Oh doesn't she look better. Work will do her good, being around her friends and having a decent conversation for a change. Have a great day Missy, you need one.

Missy has been working hard for weeks. I think she has taking her mind off Mister. He has been on a business trip a long time. He had better come back soon.

Missy is up and looking well. Her hair is beautiful and skin is glowing. A good night sleep is all she needed. The law firm she works for is so glad to have her there she has become a great asset to the firm. The firm reputation has gotten great reviews since Missy has become an attorney with the firm. Missy has worked with Bells and Grey Law firm for the past twelve years and she has loved every minute of it. Being a Criminal attorney is tough, long hours and an attorney never know who the client will be. Once she represented a Pastor of a local mega church for murdering the Choir Director. Wow what a case that was. Some nights the Pastor and his Associate Ministers would stay all night. I thought that case would never end. Missy got him cleared of the charge. She is a smart woman.

Well, off to work she goes, have a nice day Missy. I am going to sleep all day myself.

Well, Missy is home earlier than normal and I see she has guest. They're her friends from college. It has been a while since they have visited Missy. She goes in the kitchen to bring out horsderves then she goes to change her clothes. Her friends are so glad to see her. It has been months since the three of them have gotten together for a chat.

18

The women right away notice how different the family room looks. When Missy comes in one friend asked "why the changes?" Missy said she wanted the new look to be a surprise for Mister. He has been on a business trip for the past five months and this was his welcome home gift. They notice how she contrasts the colors of Italy, her home country, into the room. "We love how you represent your home country." "Oh yes, I had too, that's Mister home as well."

"Okay, how about bread with wine to start, then a rib eye steak with red potatoes with a garlic sauce, and a garden salad?" Missy goes to get the bread and wine. She put the wine on ice and places the bread on the table cloth on the coffee table.

Oh how her friends love her cooking. Missy was no stranger in the kitchen. She can whip up a meal in minutes from nothing. Missy was just enjoying herself while the girls looked at old photos and reminisce. The women start to laugh and Missy peek her head over to see what was so funny. One of the women holds up a picture of a male fraternity group and points to the guy she was head over heels about. Missy laughs too, then stops and look as if to day dream. One of the women calls her name, "Missy." The oven timer rings and Missy turns the timer off and then she say, "that was a turn never taken."

Mausilee Jackson

One of the women says," What do you mean?" Missy reply; "Well sometimes in life we miss the opportunity given to us and go another way. That's what happened to me. I missed the boat waiting for me and got on a comet waiting to destroy my life. Well I hope you two never know how that feels." "Okay dinner is served." One of the

19

women made the remark of how late it is. "It's too late to eat a meal this heavy." "Why do you Italians eat so late?" Missy says, we've always eaten dinner after eight, and not one minute early. Just enjoy."

After dinner, Missy serves chocolates and red wine. The women are in heaven. Missy says, "Not to late for chocolate is it?" Oh how the women are enjoying the night. It is good for Missy too; she's not acting like a weird person. "Well we must call this night to an end, for now." "Let's not wait so long next time." Each say they're goodbyes and hug.

Missy cleans the dishes and stove, then goes to take a shower. She is still glowing in ah from the great time she had with her friends. Missy turns on some music before getting in the shower. Oh how she is enjoying this night. I hope she is feeling better now. Missy enjoys the remainder of the night by music and candle light.

As Missy drifts off to sleep, I think she is thinking of her joyous moment with her friends and the plans and dreams she hope to conquer. Missy sleeps with a smile on her face. Off to never a bad day land. What a wonderful world that could be. Never a bad day is great.

"Good morning world. How was your night?" Missy smiles as she fixes breakfast. The sun is shining, and the wind is blowing oh such a cool breeze I feel from the kitchen window.

Missy eats then dresses for work. Today she wears a Lilac leopard print safari dress with white pumps, a pearl teardrop triple-strand necklace with earrings and a ring to match. It's been a long time since anyone has seen Missy dress like this. It is out of the norm but I

20

guess Missy wants to look good for a change.

Well Missy is home with a big smile on her face. She kicks off her pumps and says while looking in the mirror by the door in the foyer "Missy you showed them who's woman." I guess she had a great day.

Missy is a very brilliant attorney for Bells and Grey Attorney at Law. She soon will be a partner. She has won more cases than any other attorney in the firm. During her twelve years there, she has gain more prestige than the local names combined. Not only does she have a PhD degree, but Missy is just plain smart and has a gift for helping people. Missy is so excited that she had to call her friend. "Hello Brittany, Did you know the ladies in the firm were astonished at what I was wearing and one of the ladies asks, "What are your plans after work Missy?" "You look good." Missy smiles and says, "I just wanted to look different today." Then Richard Bell, who turned thirty yesterday, you remember he is Paul Bell's grandson. Well anyway he stopped by my office and asked me to see him before I leave for the day. Richard is in training to run the law firm after his father Harold Bell retires. It will be a long while before that happens."

Well I did not notice the time, it was six o'clock. I was sure I had missed Richard, but he too didn't know it was passed four. I knocked on his door, he motioned for me to come in. He was talking to a client on the computer by way of skype. I stood waiting for a sign to sit.

He never asked me to sit instead, Richard says briefly, "Meet with Mr. Paul Bells and Mrs. Fran Grey tomorrow at twelve noon at the Ice Cream Shop." "I was stunned and quietly says, "Okay, I will pencil that in on my agenda for tomorrow." Just to jog your memory

Brittany, Mrs. Grey took over the firm in place of her late husband Samuel Grey, who co-owned the firm back in 1997.

My heart was pounding and my breathing was shallow. I took a deep breath, sat quietly for a minute. I wonder what is going to happen at the meeting. I began to think back at what may have been reported. You know Brittany, I could not think of anything. So I cleaned my desk, turned off the lights and came home. Well whatever it is I can handle it. I will let you know what happens. have a great night Brittany. Goodbye." Missy goes up stairs, showers and goes to bed.

"Oh my goodness, 8 am already. I slept pretty well last night. I better start getting dress for this meeting I am to attend today."

Oh I see Missy is up and dressed. She looks very professional today. She is wearing a Navy Blue pin-stripe pant suit rocking a gold Ashley Tassel tote with gold pumps. I saw her pick that out on the internet.

Missy places her tote on the table by the sofa then goes into the kitchen to make tea and maybe eat a bagel as she normally does before going to work. Before she enters the kitchen the doorbell rings. Missy answers the door, then says; "Well what a surprise, come and have a seat." It is Mrs. Grey and Mr. Bell.

Mrs. Grey looked at Missy as if to have never seen her before. Missy says "I was told to meet with you both at the Ice Cream Soda Shop. Mrs. Grey said, "Well I did notice late last night about another meeting I had at the same time I had asked to meet with you. So we decided to come to your home instead. I hope you do not mind." Missy said " No, I do not mind at all. I was about to have tea, would you care for a tea or coffee?

22

Mrs. Grey said "Oh no dear." Mr. Bell however, looked as if to not care, but as he pulled out some paper work from his briefcase he said "no thank you." As Missy sat down, Mr. Bell did notice how beautiful she was looking. He mustard up a "hello" and Missy spoke back. The meeting began and Mrs. Grey spoke first. Mr. Bell did all the paperwork and welcomed Missy as the new Partner for Bells and Grey with a nice salary to start. Missy thanked each of them with a hand shake. Mrs. Grey arose as did Mr. Bell and Mrs. Grey said "This new position will take effect on Monday. So enjoy the weekend. Also by the way, how is your husband? Mister, am I right? Missy looked with a smile and said, "yes, that is correct and he is fine. He is out of town on business and I can not wait to tell him the good news." Mrs. Grey walks to the front door and notice the tote on the table. "Nice tote," Mrs. Grey said. "Thanks" Missy replied.

Missy was so excited she called her friends and invited them out for drinks. Missy never goes out for drinks. Missy agreed to meet the girls at eight o'clock at Willie J Cocktail Lounge. It is one o'clock in the morning and Missy finally gets home. Missy looks around the house then goes upstairs to bed.

Sunday morning and Missy wakes screaming. She is talking so fast I don't understand her. She is mad about something. Is she talking to Mister? I don't see him. I don't hear him either. Something is wrong with Missy. She looks like a different person. She looks like she didn't sleep last night. She normally goes to church, but its 12 o'clock noon and church is over. I have no idea what is wrong. I wish Mister was home at least he could help fix whatever the problem is.

23

"What do you mean I was nothing to you?" I was the best thing that happened to you. I was the one that saved you from harm. I could have made you fly. You had no idea what to do in America until I came along and helped you decide. That's what made you and I click together like a Lego block. We, so I thought, were an item, and then you changed. I was taken for granted. I was used and abused. I was treated like an old dish rag; you washed me to pieces and then tossed me in the trash. I kept you in my heart. My love for you could out weigh any hate you had for me. I was your solider. I saluted you in every adventure you tried. Who could have cared for you better? But you, you had to get ugly and start calling me names. Calling me names no husband would dare say to the one he loved. You were talking to me worse than a human talk to an animal. I never would have stoop that low and belittle you. As far as I was concerned it was just you and I in this world. Nothing or no one else mattered. I thought you were a fountain of wisdom, I drank every word from you, every advice you gave, and every direction you showed. To my dismay, you were a lie, a disappointment, and a con.

I treated you with respect that you didn't deserved. Now I know I put you on a peddle stool that was too high. I placed you in a class that a man like you would taunt.

What I done to you was not enough. I should have placed you in a catapult and beamed you into the ocean. I believe you would have founded a way to come back, as evil as you are.

Satan always returns. Cutting and burning is a satisfying solution. I may hear you, but my God I won't ever see you again.

I have learned to put up with the talks. As soon as I can figure out how to rid myself of that, I will be free."

Missy goes to bed. Thanks. That was wearing me out.

Well Missy is off to work today and looking very nice. Missy returns home looking nice with a smile on her face. She picks up the phone and calls Brittany. "Brittany, let me tell you what happened today!" "As I enter into the office this morning and to my surprise, Richard and Paul were waiting for me. "Hello Missy," they both say together. "Hello" I replied hello. Paul says, "We want to show you, your brand new office." As we walked down the hall, they each look at each other and smile. Then I stopped and looked out the window. Being a little afraid of heights it sometimes bother me, but today I enjoyed the view and the height did not seem to be a threat."

"Ten more steps and you will be in your new home as long as you want it to be." replies Richard. I walked in and to my surprise once again, it is beautiful. Cream colored walls with soft water paintings hanging like someone knew I liked the ocean. On the desk is a picture frame, which plays the sounds of the ocean, with me and Mr. Harold Bell shaking hands when I became employed with Bell and Grey Law firm.

The boarder on the walls are maroon with an outline of pink with a pink rose every six feet.

I am so stunned by the beauty of the office and with a faint voice I said "Thank you." Then Richard and Paul walk out. Before I could even sit a called by my secretary, Sophia, tells me my ten o'clock is here and I said "Give me five minutes." Okay that is all I wanted to say. I know you all were coming but I had to tell you before I exploded. See you all soon."

25

Missy change clothes and checks the mail. Then the doorbell rings. It is Jasmine, Brittany, and Susan at the door, rushing to get in. Missy says "hello, and to why do I owe this visit?" with a smile.

The girls say "hello Missy and Congratulations" " you know we heard you got your own office, no more cubical for Missy." Missy laughs and say have a seat and let's decide who is going to cook dinner. So the ladies kick off their heels and slump into the comfy couch. Missy says "someone please get the wine glasses and I will bring up some wine from the basement."

Susan goes to the kitchen and get four large wine glasses.

Jasmine see the large glasses and say "what are you trying to do, get us drunk?" "One of those glasses holds a whole bottle of wine." Susan says "no it doesn't, but if it does, I need it. I had a tornado of a day. All of my employees had an off day. They forgot the orders, served orders to wrong tables, charged the wrong amount to several customers. Computers went crazy and I thought I could handle that since I know computers but the damn things went crazy like the employees. We had to bring out Betsy. Jasmine said "not Betsy?" Susan said with a faint voice "yes." Brittany said "who is Betsy?" Jasmine said, "Girl it's the first cash register ever invented."

"Susan bought it from a retired army guy when she first opened her restaurant in 1983. The numbers are the size of a softball and a cash tray you can sleep a newborn in, it's the ugliest thing you can image. I personal think the guy invented the thing himself and color is army green. I helped her the first week of opening. Brittany shakes her

26

head and look at Susan as if too show pity."

"Okay, who is the cook for tonight?" All the ladies look at Missy and say nothing. Missy holds her head slightly downward and say "order in?" Missy grabs her cell phone and orders spaghetti with turkey balls, and a turkey sauce, garlic rolls, spinach salad, with yellow tomatoes, and apple cider dressing on the side. "Okay dinner will arrive in thirty minutes." So what happen today in your world?" The ladies look at each other and each one say, "Nothing." Now what about you and Mister? said Jasmine. Missy said "what about Mister and I?", Susan says don't get proper on us now. We know something is wrong or maybe right. We haven't figured it out yet. Where is he? How long has he been gone? Who is he working for?

Missy stands up and yell, "WHAT!?" What are you all doing? What is with all the questions? I told you at the last visit. Mister is on a business trip. He has been gone for five months. He is on an oil venture for one of the many companies he represents." "I don't remember you telling us that last time." Brittany replies.

"Well evidently you all didn't remember, you got the third degree questioner out. I am shame of you three. We are friends and you treat me like I am on trail for something gone wrong. What gives anyway?"

"Well, we have never heard of Mister being gone for this long of a time. We were worried that you and he were on bad terms and he may have gone back to Italy. We were just concerned for you. Living alone in a small community and not being able to drive." Missy interrupts "What?" "Who told you I could not drive? I can drive, I just don't like to in the city. New York scares me, it is too crowded. I prefer the cabs, it gives

27

me a chance to go over last minute notes for my cases."

Jasmine says, "What about when the church asked for van drivers and the deacon asked you, and you said No I can not drive?" Missy states "Well I meant I did not want to drive because of the city outings. You know those ladies are always going to the malls and different shopping sprees. And you know Pastor White speaks at everything New York has to open."

Are you ladies done now? Let's set the table so we can eat when the food arrive." Brittany help Missy set the table, while the other two Ladies admire the beautiful flowers from the bay window, Missy has around the patio deck and around the privacy fence. Susan says "girl I would love to have these around my windows at the restaurant." Jasmine says "they are beautiful."

Missy calls for the two to come in and eat. The ladies say grace and begin to eat. There was quietness for a while, and then Susan says,

"Your flowers are extra beautiful this season Missy. What type of soil did you use this year? It looks as if the soil has new soil mixed in it."

Missy slowly answer "yes, yes it is mixed, but I do not remember what the mixes are. I use four different types of topsoil and one potted soil. Just something I thought of, but so far so good. Oh and I used coffee grounds and left over coffee as well. It works.

Aren't these turkey balls great?" Says Missy. The ladies all say "yes" and continue to eat. They all finish eating and clear the table. Missy put a few cd's in the CD player and she starts dancing and says, "Dancing is good for the spirit ladies. Bring calmness to your inner being."

28

As the ladies look around the room they notice that most of Mister pictures are gone. Jasmine being the curious one says, "Where are all of Mister Pictures? I only see a few." Missy says "I am fixing up the basement for Mister. Mostly all of his pictures will be there for his man-cave. We decided to do this before he left. So I thought I would surprise him." Susan says, "well you better hurry, the basement has nothing in it, and Mister could be home at anytime."

Missy says "I got time, it won't take long." Susan looks at Jasmine. The two ladies walk around the room to see if they notice anything else. Brittany notice this and say to the two "stop it, I see what you are doing and I don't like it" Susan say, "because she is your best friend you don't think she has done or he has done something out of the ordinary for the two. I think other wise," Jasmine says, "I do also. I think something stinks and Missy is not her usual self."

The ladies notice new paint has been painted around the floor board and window seal, but only in a certain area, also some of the wood has been replaced with new boards. They notice because the boards do not match. Susan begins to take pictures without anyone noticing. Susan also notices that not all the flowers inside are as pretty as the outside flowers all but one. The African violet is very pretty. It has a rich deep color and the flower head is very large. The odor of the soil smells also. Susan takes a picture of the Violet. While Susan sits on the sofa, she goggle African violets and notice the flowers on goggle are not as large as Missy violet. She snapshot a picture to compare and Missy violet is twice as large. It may not be

anything but the ladies all know Missy has no green thumb. Well the ladies has had enough and want to go home. "Missy, Susan says, I think we'll go now but I maybe back soon for some tea and I'll whip you up a nice pie." Missy say, "Oh no need to hurry back. I have an awful lot to do and you know I like my naps."

"Oh I'll call before I come and you can tell me Ya or Na." "Okay" Missy said. "And leave a message if I'm not here."

Four days later the doorbell rings. Missy answers it and to her surprise it is Susan. "Susan" Missy says. "You said you would call." Susan brought a cherry pie with her, one of Missy favorites, for the visit. "Oh Missy we are friends, and friend do not have to ask to come for a visit." As Susan enters the kitchen she looks at the beautiful flowers by the fence through the window. "Oh how the roses are so large and the marigolds are so bright in color and spread almost two feet across." Missy stepped out of the kitchen and went into the dinning room to get two dessert plates. Susan just had to get some of the soil so she reached into her purse and pulled out a zip lock bag and put some soil in the bag when Missy went to get the dessert plates. "How about some white wine instead of tea Susan?" Missy says. "No I think I'll have water instead", replied Susan.

Missy says, "Why the early visit through the week?" Susan replies "I was having a baking frizzy and thought of you and how much you like cherry pie I know its your favorite." "I baked three, I ate one myself. So dig in it taste delicious if I have to say so myself. Oh my goodness, pie before dinner? we should be shame of ourselves." Replies Susan. "Well, I won't tell if you won't." Replies Missy with a giggle.

30

Missy and Susan talk a while then Susan looks at her watch and says "Oh, Missy I must go, but it was a pleasure talking with you this afternoon. We must do this again." "Sure, but next time no pie." Missy says. Susan replied, "Right." They both hug goodbye and Missy makes a cup of coffee and listen to music before bed.

Later that night, around 1am Missy wakes up screaming. "I wonder what is wrong with Missy? I did not hear anyone come in. Did Susan stay and I not see her. I might have missed it. I have missed a few things that have gone on around here. Like where is Mister? He should have been back a long time ago. It's been almost seven months, I think, and no word from him. Mister never stay away this long. Missy is screaming like she is very angry."

"Every time I turn a corner, there you are. Why can't you go to the hole that was made for you? I remembered when you chased me down for a date. You founded out I had some money and you were like a dog chasing a car. Every time I looked up, there you were. You jumped on this float before the parade started, trying to beat another man to the point. Well guess what? The parade is over and the float is dismembered. So go rock some other fool world. My dream was always bigger than you and you hated it. You hated the fact that I can make it without you. You wanted me to depend on you, but I knew I would not ever do that. Some nights when you tried to go to the promise land on me, you would not put passion into it. You wanted to hit and miss, but you missed my la-la every time.

The love we shared was not important to you. You didn't need the love I had. My roses were too ripe for you and your foundation had a

flaw that was unrepairable. It was then I knew your tower was ending. I want to thank you for degrading me. Thanks for belittling and shaming me. You made me a stronger and much better woman. Now I, Ms. Missy can shine. So move you evil rotten thing no one need. I can't live your life. I must let the world know I made this life on my own. You gave me nothing. Oh yes you did, I forgot. You gave me heartache and pains, baldness and shot nerves. But I renounce your admission in my life anymore.

My life was a Pandora's Box with you. I never knew what was behind the smile on your face or the kiss on my cheek. I had to be on my toes at all times and man did the tips of my shoes wear out. I kept a secret weapon with me at all times. I notice it does not work anymore but I soon will find out what will work to get rid of you.

I am worth more than you can ever count. You will never find a ruby like me. I shine like sun in the day and the moon at night. I shine like the twinkle of the stars in the sky. You could not hang with me. My IQ was too much for you to compare with. I was finished with the paragraph before you could read the first sentence. The more I think this over, you need to leave. Now, would be nice."

"Oh, I am so glad last night is over. Who can sleep when Missy is in that mood? How can she deal with today?

There is a knock on the back door. Missy looks out the window and she see two strange men. She hesitates to open the door but opens it slowly. She barley opens where the men can see her face and one man holds up a badge and say."

"Hello We are the FBI, I am Agent John and this is Agent Brown.

32

We have had a complaint about an odor coming from your back yard. Do you mind if we just look around?"

Missy says, "do you have a warrant?" The two look at each other and politely say, "No, we do not. This was just a look around no biggie." Well if you want to look, you need the proper paperwork please. I have no problem with you looking. You just need to have the right credentials. Good day Gentlemen."

Missy goes to the kitchen table. She has an odd look on her face.

She fixes a cup of coffee and sits and drinks. Missy walks over to the window where the flowers are and she notices a dip in the soil. Missy says, "that's funny. Look like some soil has been taken out, but why?" Missy takes a picture of the flower soil. While looking out the window she notices the same dip in the flowerbed. Missy goes outside to look closer and notice the same dip trace. Missy takes a picture of the flowerbed.

Missy goes to the computer and scans the pictures to take a closer look. She notices that each dip looks just alike. Missy goes to look at the other flower pots to see if there was a dip in those as well. But there wasn't one. So Missy goes to look at the pictures again to make sure she was looking at the picture correct. Then the phone rings and Missy did not answer it nor did she turn on the answering machine. Missy is in a daze. She wonders how this can be. So she finishes her coffee and gets dress for the day. It's Saturday, a day to unwind and relax. Missy may go shopping, but just as she walks to the door, Susan is at the door.

33

Susan says; "Well hello, my lady. How are you this fine day Love?" Missy say "Susan you hang with the UK men too much. You're beginning to sound like one. Why are you here today Susan?".

"Well the sun is shinning and the air is cool. I thought we could go for brunch in the park. What do you say?" Missy said, "No Susan. After that pie last week I need to stay away from you and food for a while." Susan replied, "Oh, we don't have to eat sweets but there is a food truck over there that serves the green way. Smoothies, soups, tofu all healthy food."

"No. I have earrings to run today and I would like to get them done earlier. So maybe next time Susan." "Okay, have a wonderful day. Enjoy your earring run. Oh, have you heard from Mister yet?" Susan ask. Missy replied "Oh he called and said he was delayed again and would call when he get a chance." "Okay I'd thought I'd ask. Take care Love." replied Susan

Missy states "That Susan is a spy at heart. I would hate to be her brain its too crowed." Missy stares out the window. She notice the fall leaves are falling. "Oh how beautiful the trees are. I love the outdoors. Make me think of heaven." Missy walks around the kitchen and sit at the island where she can see out the front window. Missy notice Susan back in her drive again.

Missy almost yelled for her but then thought; "What is she up to?" I better wait and see. Missy step behind the bookcase tall enough to hide her. It's not long before Susan drives off. Missy continues to hide behind the bookcase then she looks around thinking as if something was disturbing her. "What the heck is going on around here?"

Suddenly, Missy says "I wonder if Susan is messing around in my

34

flowers and for what?" Missy begins to water the flowers with salt water and baking soda. Missy finishes watering the flowers and then decides to take a shower and get ready for bed. After showering, Missy boil water for tea and while the water is boiling she walks over to the flowers by the window and look around, as she look she notice there is something by the flowers beside the door. Missy steps over to look. There by the flowers is a salt and pepper shaker. Missy look stunned and say "why is there salt and pepper shakers by the flowers?" Missy turns on the cd player to do some meditation.

The water for the tea is whistling, so Missy goes to the kitchen and turn the pot off. She put water in her mug and a tea bag. She goes over by the buffet and stands there looking. She then notice the salt and pepper shakers that were placed on top as a display with the other knick-knacks were not there. "Surely no." Then Missy looks at the top and sure enough there was an empty spot by the dolphin butter dish that was her mother's dish and was given to Missy before her mother died. Missy soon tries and put all this together but having no luck at this time. Missy drinks the tea, turns off the cd player and goes to bed.

Mausilee Jackson

"What do you mean you'll be back?" Missy is talking to herself again. Well at least we got some sleep last night. It is morning maybe she will not be so angry this day. "Be back for what? Who want you no good for nothing? The ground can't hold you down but I got something for you this time." Missy goes to the kitchen and opens the broom closet and pulls out a shotgun, a double-barrel shotgun. OH MY GOODNESS! What is happening in here?

35

Missy starts shooting up the house. She starts with the flowers by the window and the she steps just outside the door and aims at the flowerbed by the fence and just starts shooting. Then she comes back into the house and shoots again.

Just as she starts to reload the two men that were here last week were back and this time they do not need the paperwork Missy insisted the have. They draw their guns on Missy and she begins to laugh. Then she put the gun down and falls to the floor and begins to cry. What is happening here? Why are they putting Missy in hand cuffs? One of the men says, Missy Tortorello "You are under arrest for the murder of Angelo Tortorello." Missy says, "my name is Missy Salvino Tortorello." Then the man says, "you have the right to remain silent, anything you say can or will be and I have no idea what else he said as he take Missy to the car outside.

But wait, did I hear correct? he said murder. But who, where, what? Missy murdered Mister? When did she do that? Oh my goodness. While Missy was away some people came and dug in the dirt by the door, putting dirt in glass bottles and searching in the flower pots as well.

Missy is home now. She looks tired. She goes upstairs and take a shower. Just as she goes into the kitchen the doorbell ring. Missy answers it.

"Missy Salvino Tortorello, I am Morgan Pruitt and I have some questions to ask you." "Sure, come in and have a seat." " Would you like a cup of tea?" Mr. Pruitt says "no thank you"

The one hundred question starts and Missy remains calm and

36

listen never saying a word to Mr. Pruitt and then Missy say "I want to call a lawyer." Mr. Pruitt gathers his papers and walk out quietly. But a policeman comes in and tells Missy she has to come with him to the station. Missy say "I need to make a call first."

Missy calls Brittany and tells her she will be getting arrested and she needs her. Brittany gets Missy out of jail. They both go to the kitchen and Brittany get some wine glasses and pour some wine and then Brittany tells Missy that when she asked the clerk what is the charge and the clerk says murder. "I felt light-headed all of a sudden, and almost faints. Then when I asked to see you and I am escorted to the room where you are drinking coffee and relaxing like nothing is happening. I hug you and says, Well Missy what is going on?" And you say "you're the lawyer you tell me." "Well you are charge with murder. Who did you murder, and you say with a smile on your face, "Mister." "I completely forgot all words."

"So now lets get to work. The judge is very tough. She doesn't play with murderers. In fact she hates people who kill other people.

I will try and see if I can make a deal with Judge Blonzia Thaman instead of the prosecutors. The judge is up for re-election and she will try to make an impression with this trail. No person that comes in her court room will walk free. Judge Thama likes to think she is supporting the criminal by locking them up. The trail date is very soon and Missy you have been very quiet about this murder charge. Did you know Susan has been talking to the FBI and has not visited you one time?"

37

Missy face has changed. She has been meditating and speaking to her pastor a lot. In fact most of the church members have visit Missy and sent cards and letters to comfort her.

"Well Missy are you ready? We need to be at the court house in two hours. Missy you will be escorted to the court house by the police." Missy comes down stairs dressed in her favorite color pant suit, purple trimmed in gold. The officer let Brittany know they are out front and when they are ready to leave Missy will have to be placed in handcuffs. Brittany looks at Missy and Missy nod as to say okay.

Missy says to Brittany "Are you comfortable?" Brittany looks at the paperwork and then says quietly "yes."

Just then the officer comes in and say "Judge Blonzia Thaman is coming up the drive." Brittany says, "let her in." The Judge comes inside and stands there for a minute and look at the surrounding then she sits. After everyone is seated Judge Thaman looks at the paperwork on her lap, it was so quiet in the room you could hear only breathing. Then Judge Thaman looks up and ask; "Brittany Boyd have you had ample time to prepare for this case?"

Brittany says "yes your Honor." Judge says "This is not going to be easy on you Ms. Boyd. Mrs. Tortorello is your best friend. I am worried you do not know all there is to know of her. Listening to witnesses, some you never heard of and some you two are close too, and looking at pictures yes pictures. I am ordering that this case be rested in three days and then the attorney's will give their closing

statement. Officer take this woman to the court house and lets begin."

Three days and the case was over. Five hours has passed and the jury has reached a verdict. The Officer stands by the front door as if he was guarding it. The court room is on video so Missy would not have to go to the court house for the verdict. Missy looks like she is okay with whatever happens. The verdict is read, "Not Guilty." and everyone screams and cries and hugs Missy. Missy is crying and she hugs Brittany. Then Missy goes into the kitchen and looks up to the skylight and whisper, "Ti amo Angelo" (I love you, Angelo.)

The officer comes in the house and say, "Judge Blonzia Thaman would like to see you Mrs. Tortorello." Missy says, "Sure"

The Judge comes in and hugs Missy and shake Brittany hand and nod then walks out. Brittany say to Missy " I guess we have a friend for life." Missy say "That one is good to have."